Air Fryer Cookbook 2021

The Ultimate Collection of Quick, & Easy Air Fryer Recipes to Master the Full Potential of Your Appliance While Losing Weight

Mary Carton

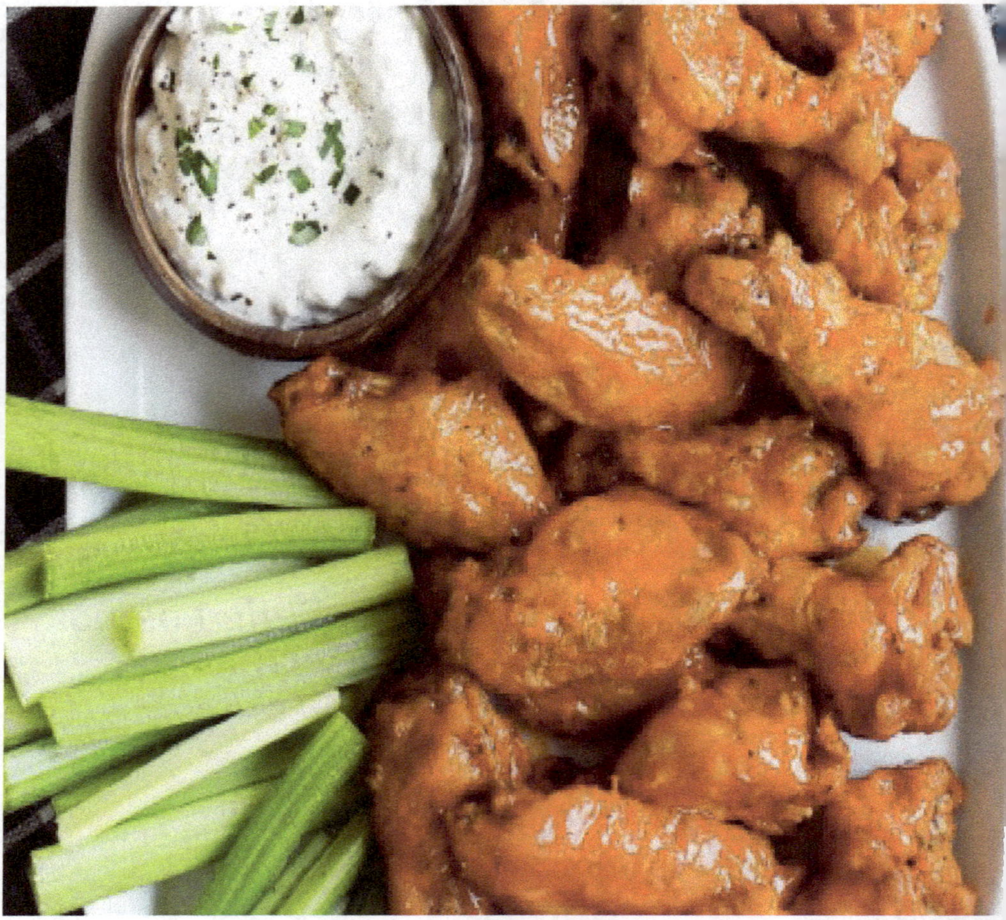

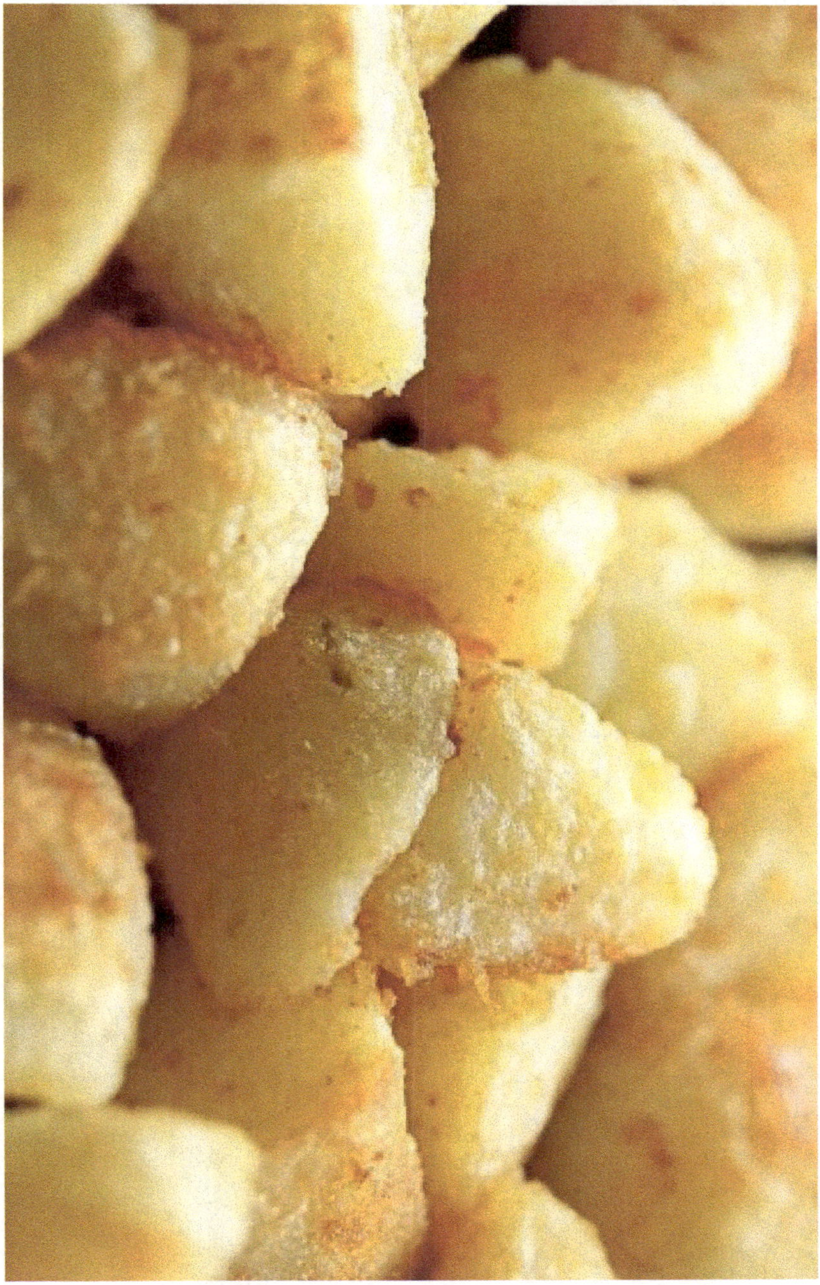

Copyright © 2020 by Mary Carton

All rights reserved. No part of this guide may be reproduced in any form without permission in writing from the publisher, except for brief quotations used for publishable articles or reviews.

Legal Disclaimer

The information contained in this book and its contents is not designed to replace any form of medical or professional advice; and is not meant to replace the need for independent medical, financial, legal, or other professional advice or services that may be required. The content and information in this book have been provided for educational and entertainment purposes only.

The content and information contained in this book have been compiled from sources deemed reliable, and they are accurate to the best of the Author's knowledge, information, and belief. However, the Author cannot guarantee its accuracy and validity and therefore cannot be held liable for any errors and/or omissions. Further, changes are periodically made to this book as needed. Where appropriate and/or necessary, you must consult a professional (including but not limited to your doctor, attorney, financial advisor, or other such professional) before using any of the suggested remedies, techniques, and/or information in this book.

Upon using this book's contents and information, you agree to hold harmless the Author from any damages, costs, and expenses, including any legal fees potentially resulting from the application of any of the information in this book. This disclaimer applies to any loss, damages, or injury caused by the use and application of this book's contents, whether directly or indirectly, whether for breach of contract, tort, negligence, personal injury, criminal intent, or under any other circumstance.

Table of Contents

The Basics of Air Fryer 12
What is an Air Fryer? 12
Having a look at how the Air Fry works 13
Core features of the Air Fryer 13
Cleaning And Maintenance 15
Amazing advantages of the Air Fryer 16
Essential troubleshooting guide 18
General cooking timetable 18

RECIPES 21
Potato Pancakes 21
Quinoa Eggplant Rolls 23
Peas With Mushrooms 25
Buffalo Cauliflower Bites 27
Very "Salty" Parsnips 29
Hearty Rosemary Munchies 31
Apple Hash brown 33
Awesome Squash Noodles 35
Delicious Apple Pie 37
Fried Pineapple Bites 39
Banana Fritter 41
Almond Apple Treat 43
Black And White Brownies 45

Apricot Crumbles	47
Nuts And Cocoa Bombs	50
Creamy Coconut Chips	52
Lovely Plum Cake	53
Divine Almond Cupcakes	55
Terrific Baked Plum	57
Hearty Currant Pudding	58
Spicy Avocado Pudding	59
Authentic Chocolate Mug Cake	61
Cinnamon And Cheese Pancake	63
Scallops And Dill	65
Cheesy Bread Cups	67
Peanut Butter And Banana Sandwich	69
Mini Cheeseburger Sliders	71
Chicken Cheese Fillet	73
Pineapple Pizza	75
Lovely Plum Cream	77
Air Fried Spinach Fish	78
Tandori Fish	80
Cod And Fennel Meal	82
Prawn Curry	84
Crusted Halibut	86
Spiced Up Air Fried Buffalo Wings	88
Caprese Chicken With Balsamic Sauce	90
Rice Flour Crusted Tofu	92
Healthy Croissant Rolls	94

Cheesy Mushroom Pizza 96
Chinese Mushroom Tilapia 98
Air Fried Dragon Shrimp 100
Stuffed Breadcrumbs Mushrooms 102
Basil Dip And Assorted Roast Vegetable 104
Warm Chickpea Burger 106
Exceptional Spaghetti Squash Roast 108
Spiced Up Orange Bowl 110
Exquisite Squash Salad 112

The Basics of Air Fryer

Before diving deep into the recipes themselves, I think we must have an understanding of the individual appliances that we are working with here. Since this book has a vast compilation of 900+ recipes that span a multitude of appliances, having a good understanding of each of them will help you get the best out of each of the recipes!

That being said, let's start with the most question first,

What is an Air Fryer?

To keep things short and straightforward, Air Fryer is one of the most unique and innovative appliances to hit the market!

This is an excellent cooking appliance that utilizes the power of superheated "Air" and carefully placed exhaust fans to evenly distribute hot air around the food and perfectly cook the meal, with minimal oil usage!

Upon its release, the Air Fryer broke some boundaries and became an instant hit. It's popularity reached such levels that even Gordon Ramsay took notice and claimed that "Air Is The New Oil."

The cooking mechanism of the device is what makes it so "Unique."

While other kitchen appliances tend to rely on the technique of conduction mostly, Air Fryers differentiate themselves from the crow by implementing the flow of air into the cooking process and cook the meals through the method of "Convection."

Using Air, and the so-called "Rapid Air Technology," which I have talked about in the next section.

Having a look at how the Air Fry works

Now that you have a good idea of what the Air Fryer is let me briefly breakdown how the Air Fryer works.

Well, it's pretty simple if you think about it.

The keyword here is "Air."

Most other conventional cooking appliances tend to cook their meal by using some sort of heater that passes heat through the meal through a process known as conduction. This transfers heat to the meal in touch.

An Air Fryer, on the other hand, does its cooking through a process called "Convection," where the air is heated up and circulated throughout the food.

During your journey into the various supermarkets looking for an Air Fryer, you have most definitely seen the word "Rapid Air Technology" countless times. That refers to a very delicately designed process that the Air Fryer uses to cook its food.

The Air has sucked up the intake chamber, and the appliance gets heated up.

Core features of the Air Fryer

You should understand that different Air Fryer companies will try to include special features of their own. Still, the following are the most general elements that you may expect to find in all Air Fryers out there.

- **Automated Temperature Control System:** The automatic temperature control system allows the appliance to keep track of the temperature and turn off the system when the airflow reaches a specific temperature. This allows every meal to be created according to the user's personal preferences.
- **Digital Screen and Touch Panel:** Air Fryers have implemented a full touch screen that greatly helps the newcomers to easily adjust themselves with the new appliance and start cooking right away using the pre-set heat settings and other functionalities.
- **A Convenient Buzzer:** The Buzzer and Timer of Air Fryers allow individuals to easily know when their dish is ready, thanks to the buzzing sound which the device makes when the timer runs out.
- **An Assorted Selection of Cooking Presets:** The Air Fryer comes packed with a large array of pre-set cooking programs that helps to an inexperienced chef to meals using an Air Fryer with ease.

PRESET BUTTON COOKING CHART		
PRESET BUTTON	TEMPERATURE	TIME
French Fries	400°F	20 min
Roasts	370°F	15 min
Shrimp	330°F	15 min
Baked Goods	350°F	25 min
Chicken	380°F	25 min
Steak	380°F	25 min
Fish	390°F	25 min

Cleaning And Maintenance

The longevity of your appliance largely depends on how you take care of the appliance itself in the long run. Over time, dirt and debris might accumulate on the various parts of the appliance. You must keep your Air Fryer in tip shape to ensure that it can provide you with the best performance and output possible.

While cleaning your device, you should follow the following steps for maximum efficiency!

- Make sure to remove the power cable from the outlet
- Wipe the external part of the fryer using a moist cloth dipped in mild detergent
- Clean the cooking basket and Fryer Tray with hot water and a soft sponge (dipped in mild detergent)
- Clean the inner parts using hot water and soft sponge (similarly dipped in mild detergent)
- Brush the heating element carefully to clear out any stuck residue

Amazing advantages of the Air Fryer

With all of that being said, there are many reasons as to why you should buy an Air Fryer! Below are just some of the amazing benefits that you might expect while using the Air Fryer!

- The Air Fryer is an extremely versatile appliance that will allow you to not only Air Fry dishes but also grill, roast, or even bake them as well!

- The enclosure of the Air Fryer is constructed keeping the safety of its users as the top priority, and it eliminates the risk of having hot oil falling over your skin

- The appliance is extremely easy and simple to use. The minimal use of oil results in very little built of debris/grease, which is very seamless to clean as well

- The pre-installed smart programs of the appliance are very carefully designed to help even amateur chefs prepare premium quality dishes

- Since you are cooking with superheated air here, the Air Fryer helps to save a lot of time, freeing up more of your day to spend with the people you love, and doing the things that you love

- Using the Air Fryer cuts down almost 8-85% of total oil consumption, which makes it great for your heart in the long run

- The relatively compact size and versatility of the Air Fryer means that you can easily install it in any corner of your kitchen (given it gets proper airflow) and free up space to keep your kitchen sleek and clean looking

And those are just the tip of the iceberg!

Essential troubleshooting guide

If this is your first time using the Air Fryer, it is extremely normal that you might experience troubles during your early days. The following is a very brief troubleshooting guide that

General cooking timetable

While this book already has the required temperature specified in all of the recipes, it is still important to know the general cooking temperatures of different ingredients, as it will help you significantly when trying to come up with your very own masterpieces!

Meat

	Cooking Temperature (Fahrenheit)	Cooking Time (Minutes)
Bacon	350	8-12
Chicken (Whole)	350	45-65
Chicken Breasts (Bone-In)	375	25-35
Chicken Breasts (Boneless)	350	15-20
Chicken Tenders	350	8-12
Chicken Thighs (Bone-In)	400	15-22
Chicken Thighs (Boneless)	375	16-21
Chicken Wings	375	18-28
Lamb (Leg)	375	18-28
Lamb (Rack)	375	10-17
NY Strip Steak	400	8-14
Pork Chops	350	10-15
Pork Tenderloin	375	15-25
Ribeye/T-Bone	400	15-25

Ground Meat

	Cooking Temperature (Fahrenheit)	Cooking Time (Minutes)
Burger Patties (1/4 lb)	350	8-15
Meatballs	375	6-9
Sausages (raw)	375	15-20
Sausages (cooked)	375	7-12

Chopped Sea/Food

	Cooking Temperature (Fahrenheit)	Cooking Time (Minutes)
Chicken	400	8-15
Pork	375	8-12
Steak	400	8-12
Salmon	400	6-12
Tilapia	350	6-10

Others

	Cooking Temperature (Fahrenheit)	Cooking Time (Minutes)
Banana, sliced	375	6-8
Chickpeas	400	12-17
Tofu, cubed	375	12-17
Tortilla chips	350	3-8
Pizza, personal size	375	7-12

Frozen Food

	Cooking Temperature (Fahrenheit)	Cooking Time (Minutes)
Chicken Tenders, breaded and pre-cooked	375	14-18
Dumplings/Potstickers	400	6-10
Egg Rolls	350	8-14
Fish Sticks	400	8-12
French Fries	400	14-17
Hash Browns	325	6-9
Mini Pizzas	375	8-15
Mozzarella Sticks	375	7-10
Onion Rings	400	8-10
Tater Tots	400	10-15

RECIPES

Potato Pancakes

Serving: 4

Prep Time: 10 minutes

Cook Time: 24 minutes

Ingredients:

- 4 medium potatoes, peeled and cleaned
- 1 medium onion, chopped
- 1 beaten egg
- ¼ cup milk
- 2 tablespoons unsalted butter
- ½ teaspoon garlic powder
- ¼ teaspoon salt
- 3 tablespoon all-purpose flour
- Black pepper to taste

Directions:

1. Peel your potatoes and soak them underwater.
2. Drain the potatoes to remove the starch and shred them.

3. Take a bowl and add eggs, milk, butter, pepper, garlic powder, and salt.
4. Mix well and add flour.
5. Add the potatoes and mix well.
6. Pre-heat your Air Fryer to 390 degrees Fahrenheit.
7. Take the batter and scoop up potato pancakes into the basket (each cake takes about ¼ cup of batter).
8. Cook for 12 minutes.
9. Enjoy!

Nutrition Values (Per Serving)

- Calories: 255
- Fat: 8g
- Carbohydrates: 42g
- Protein: 7g

Quinoa Eggplant Rolls

Serving: 4

Prep Time: 10 minutes

Cook Time: 15 minutes

Ingredients:

- 2 eggplants
- 3 and ½ ounces feta cheese
- 2 tablespoons olive oil
- ½ lemon juice
- 1 teaspoon ground coriander
- 1 and ¾ ounces carrot, grated
- ½ teaspoon turmeric
- 1 and ½ ounces quinoa

Directions:

1. Pre-heat your Air Fryer to 360 degrees F.
2. Wash your eggplants thoroughly and slice eggplants.
3. Take a bowl and mix in quinoa, feta cheese, sliced carrots, coriander, lemon juice, and cover with olive oil.
4. Transfer feta mix to eggplant slices.

5. Roll eggplant slices and transfer to your Air Fryer Cooking Basket.
6. Bake for 15 minutes.
7. Serve and enjoy!

Nutrition Values (Per Serving)

- Calories: 305
- Fat: 20g
- Carbohydrates: 0g
- Protein: 10g

Peas With Mushrooms

Serving: 4

Prep Time: 10 minutes

Cook Time: 10-15 minutes

Ingredients:

- 16-oz cremini mushrooms halved
- 4 garlic cloves, finely chopped
- 1/2 cup soy sauce
- 1/2 cup frozen peas
- 4 tbsp. maple syrup
- 4 tbsp. rice vinegar
- 1/2 tsp. ground ginger
- 2 tsp. Chinese five-spice powder

Directions:

1. In a bowl, mix well soy sauce, maple syrup, vinegar, garlic, five-spice powder,

and ground ginger. Set the temperature of the Air fryer to 350°F.
2. Grease your cooking basket
3. Arrange mushroom into the prepared air fryer pan in a single layer. Air fry for about 10 minutes.
4. Remove from the air fryer and stir the mushrooms.
5. Add the peas and vinegar mixture and stir to combine. Air fry for about 5 more minutes.
6. Remove from the air fryer and transfer the mushroom mixture onto serving plates. Serve hot.

Nutrition Contents:

- Calories: 437
- Fat: 20g
- Carbohydrates: 40g
- Protein: 23g

Buffalo Cauliflower Bites

Serving: 6

Prep Time: 5 minutes

Cook Time: 5-8 minutes

Ingredients

- 3 ounce of cauliflower finely sliced 12mm thick florets
- 1 tablespoon of olive oil
- Kosher Salt
- Freshly ground pepper

Directions

1. Pre-heat your Air Fryer to 390 degrees Fahrenheit
2. Take a bowl and toss cauliflower, olive oil and season with a bit of salt and pepper
3. Take your frying basket and add the cauliflowers
4. Fry for 5-6 minutes, making sure to shake them halfway through
5. Once done, take the cauliflowers out and serve them
6. Enjoy!

Nutritional Contents:

- Calories: 240.9

- Fat: 5.5g
- Carbohydrates: 6.2g
- Protein: 8.8g

Very "Salty" Parsnips

Serving: 2

Prep Time: 5 minutes

Cook Time: 15 minutes

Ingredients:

- 3 Parsnips
- 2-ounce almond flour
- 1 cup of water
- 2 tablespoon olive oil
- Salt as needed

Directions:

1. Peel the parsnips and slice them up into French Fry shapes
2. Take a bowl and add water, , salt, , olive oil and almond flour
3. Mix well
4. Add the parsnips and coat them evenly
5. Pre-heat your Fryer to 400 degrees Fahrenheit
6. Add parsnips to the Air Fryer and cook for 15 minutes
7. Serve and enjoy!

Nutrition Values (Per Serving)

- Calories: 228
- Carbohydrate: 15g
- Protein: 4g
- Fat: 17g

Hearty Rosemary Munchies

Serving: 6

Prep Time: 30 minutes

Cook Time: 30 minutes

Ingredients:

- 4 medium-sized russet potatoes
- 1 tablespoon of olive oil
- 2 teaspoon of finely chopped rosemary
- 2 pinches of salt

Directions:

1. Scrub your potatoes well and wash them underwater
2. Cut the potatoes into chip shapes
3. Soak the potatoes underwater for about 30 minutes
4. Drain the potatoes and place them on a kitchen towel
5. Pre-heat your Air Fryer to 330 degrees Fahrenheit
6. Take a bowl and add olive oil, potatoes, and mix
7. Transfer the potatoes to your Air Fryer and cook for 30 minutes until you have a nice golden brown texture
8. Give it a nice shake
9. Season and serve!

Nutrition Values (Per Serving)

- Calories: 593
- Carbohydrate: 0g
- Protein: 2g
- Fat: 39g

Apple Hash brown

Serving: 2

Prep Time: 10 minutes

Cooking Time: 20 minutes

Ingredients:

- 1 sweet potato, chopped
- 1 apple, chopped
- 1 teaspoon ground cinnamon
- 1 tablespoon olive oil

Directions:

1. Pre-heat your Air Fryer 380 degrees F
2. Add oil and add chopped sweet potatoes, cook for 15 minutes
3. Add chopped apple, ground cinnamon and stir well, cook for 5 minutes more
4. Stir and enjoy it!

Nutritional Contents:

- Calories: 172
- Fat: 9g
- Carbohydrates: 28g

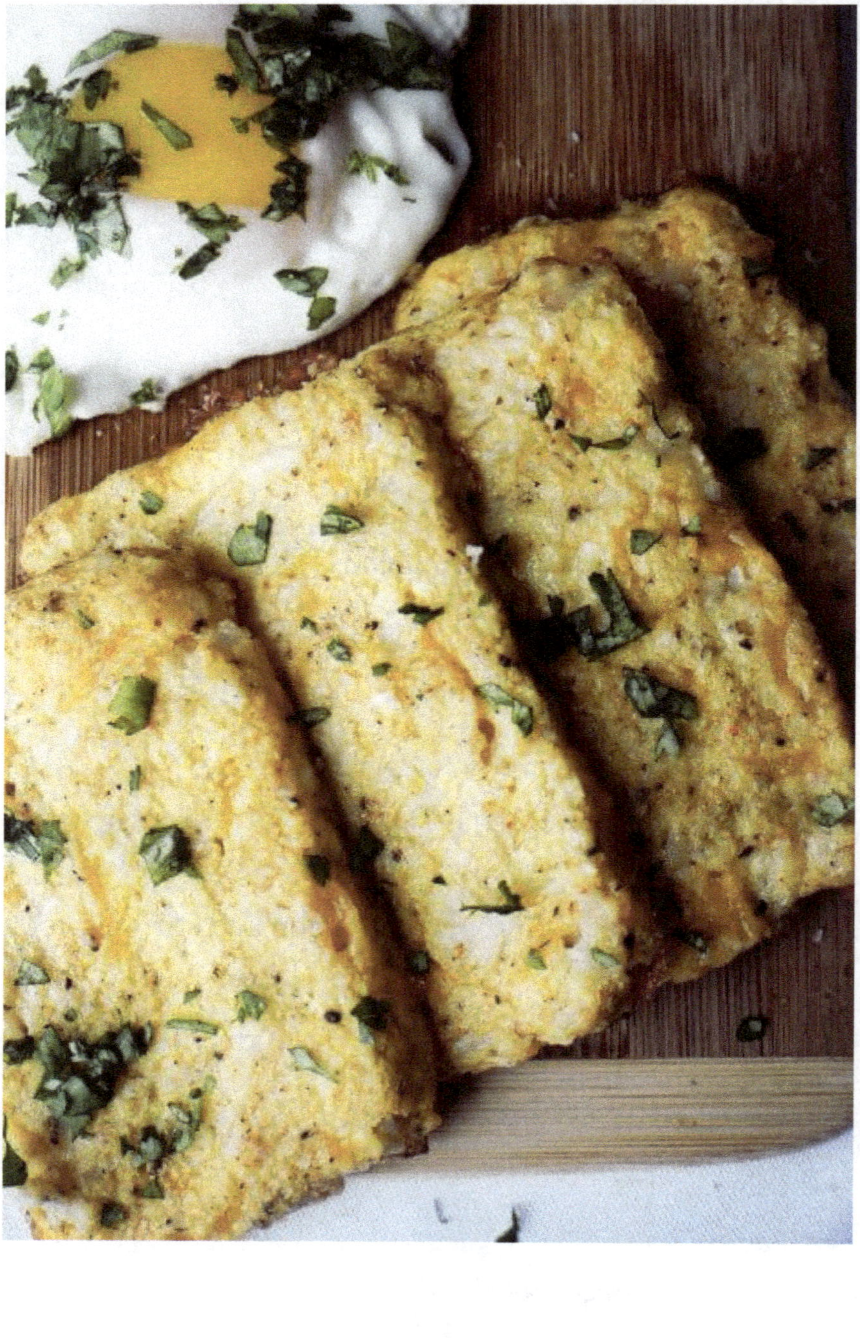

Awesome Squash Noodles

Serving: 2

Prep Time: 10 minutes

Cooking Time: 20 minutes

Ingredients:

- 15 ounces spaghetti squash
- 1 tablespoon olive oil
- ½ teaspoon dried dill
- ½ teaspoon salt

Directions:

1. Peel spaghetti squash and transfer to Air Fryer
2. Cook for 15 minutes at 390 degrees F
3. Shred squash with a fork and make noodles
4. Transfer squash noodles to bowl and sprinkle olive oil, dried dill, and salt
5. Stir in noodles, serve and enjoy!

Nutritional Contents:

- Calories: 63.7
- Fat: 5g
- Carbohydrates: 7g

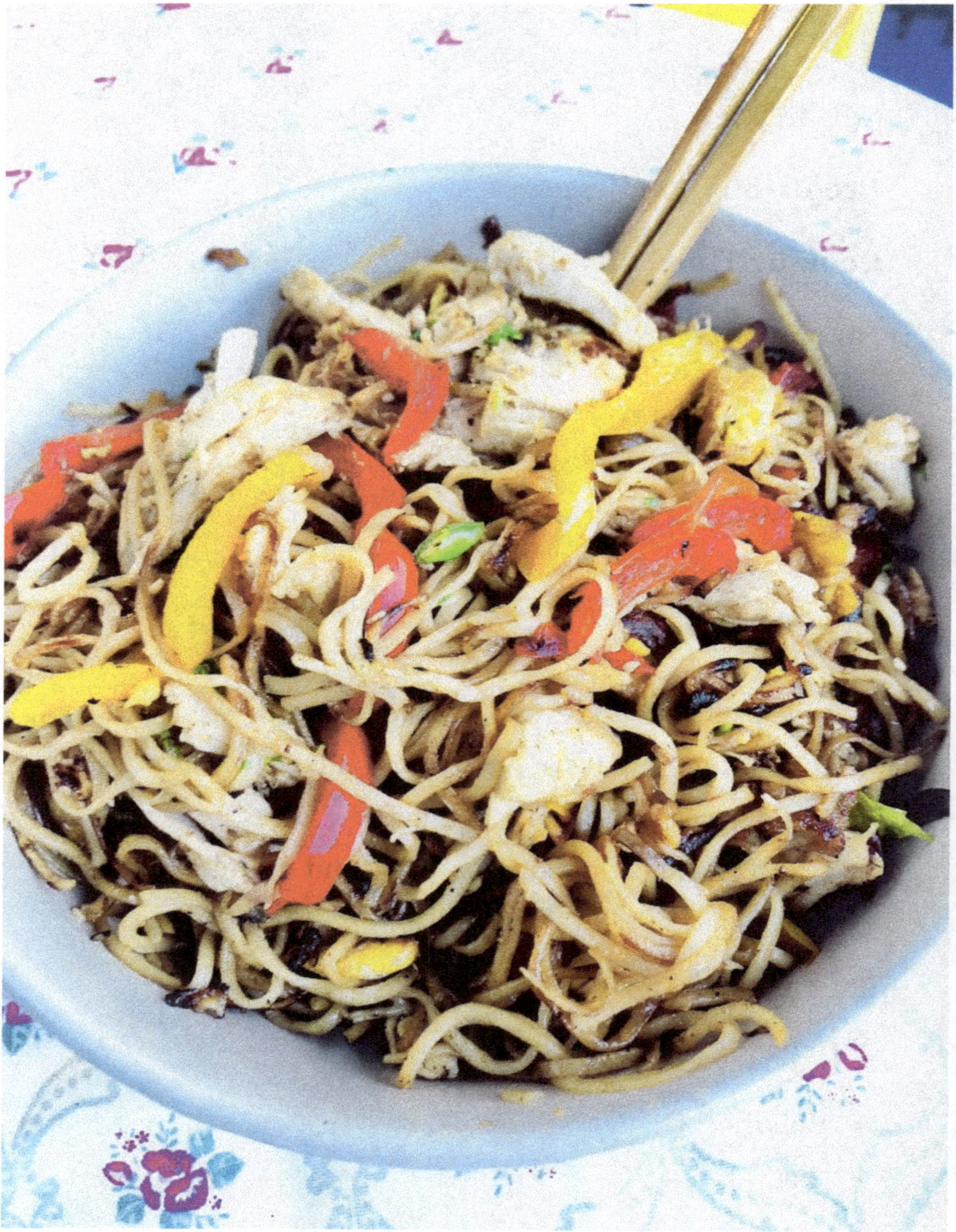

Delicious Apple Pie

Serving: 5

Prep Time: 5 minutes

Cook Time: 20 minutes

Ingredients:

- 2 and ¾ ounces flour
- 5 tablespoons sugar
- 1 and ¼ ounces butter
- 3 tablespoons cinnamon
- 2 whole apples

Directions:

1. Pre-heat your Air Fryer to 360 degrees F.
2. Take a bowl and mix in 3 tablespoons sugar, butter, and flour.
3. Form the pastry.
4. Wash and cut apples.
5. Cover apples with sugar and cinnamon.
6. Lay apples on your pastry and cover with dough.
7. Place pie in your Fryer and cook for 20 minutes.
8. Serve with sprinkles of powdered sugar and fresh mint.
9. Enjoy!

Nutrition Values (Per Serving)

- Calories: 223
- Fat: 8g
- Carbohydrates: 37g
- Protein: 2g

Fried Pineapple Bites

Serving: 4

Prep Time: 5 minutes

Cook Time: 15 minutes

Ingredients:

- 3-4 pieces of Raw Banana
- 1 teaspoon of Salt
- ½ a teaspoon of Turmeric Powder
- ½ a teaspoon of Chaat Masala
- 1 teaspoon of olive oil

Directions:

1. Cut the pineapple in half and take the skin away, remove the crowns
2. Take out the inner core cut in half again into 4 wedges
3. Pre-heat your Fryer to 352 degrees Fahrenheit
4. Brush the lime juice all over the pineapple
5. Transfer the pineapple to your Air Fryer
6. Sprinkle coconut shreds on top and cook for 12 minutes
7. Serve!

<u>Nutrition Values (Per Serving)</u>

- Calories: 467
- Fat: 12g
- Carbohydrates: 10g
- Protein: 7g

Banana Fritter

Serving: 5

Prep Time: 5 minutes

Cooking Time: 8 minutes

Ingredients:

- 1 and ½ cups flour
- 5 bananas, peeled and sliced
- 1 teaspoon salt
- 3 tablespoon sesame seeds
- 1 cup of water

Directions:

1. Pre-heat your Air Fryer to 340 degrees F.
2. Take a bowl and add salt, sesame seeds, water, and mix well.
3. Coat bananas with the flour mixture and transfer to the Air Fryer basket.
4. Cook for 8 minutes.
5. Serve and enjoy!

Nutritional Contents:

- Calories: 242
- Fat: 9g
- Carbohydrates: 38g
- Protein: 5g

Almond Apple Treat

Serving: 4

Prep Time: 15 minutes

Cooking Time: 20 minutes

Ingredients:

- 4 apples
- 1 and ½ ounces almonds
- Whipped cream
- ¾ ounces raisins
- 2 tablespoons sugar

Directions:

1. Pre-heat your Air Fryer to 360 degrees F.

2. Wash apples and clean, cut off the cores.

3. Take a bowl and mix in sugar, almonds, raisins. Blend using a blender.

4. Fill apples with the almond mixture.

5. Cook apples in Fryer for 10 minutes.

6. Serve with powdered sugar, enjoy!

Nutritional Contents:

- Calories: 200
- Fat: 24g
- Carbohydrates: 33g
- Protein: 5g

Black And White Brownies

Serving: 4

Prep Time: 10 minutes

Cooking Time: 20 minutes

Ingredients:

- 1 whole egg
- ¼ cup of chocolate chips
- 2 tablespoons white sugar
- 1/3 cup flour
- 2 tablespoons safflower oil
- 1 teaspoon vanilla
- ¼ cup of cocoa powder

Directions:

1. Pre-heat your Fryer to 320 degrees F.
2. Take a bowl and mix in the beaten egg with brown sugar, white sugar, oil, and vanilla Mix cocoa powder with flour and add to the sugar mix.
3. Prepare a baking form for your Air Fryer.
4. Pour the brownie dough in your Air Fryer and cook for 20 minutes.
5. Serve with ice-cream.
6. Enjoy!

Nutritional Contents:

- Calories: 470
- Fat: 13g
- Carbohydrates: 30g
- Protein: 2g

Apricot Crumbles

Serving: 4

Prep Time: 10 minutes

Cooking Time: 20 minutes

Ingredients:

- 2 and ½ cups fresh apricot
- 1 cup fresh blackberries
- ½ cup of sugar
- 2 tablespoons lemon juice
- 1 cup flour
- Salt as needed
- 5 tablespoons butter

Directions:

1. Cut apricots in half and remove the stones.
2. Cut the halves in cubes and add them to a bowl.
3. Add lemon juice, 2 tablespoons sugar, blackberries, to the bowl and mix.
4. Scoop the mixture into a greased dish and spread.
5. Take another bowl and add flour and remaining sugar.
6. Add 1 tablespoon of cold water and butter to the mix and keep mixing until you have a crumbly mixture.

7. Pre-heat your Air Fryer to 390 degrees F.

8. Distribute the crumb mix on top of fruit and transfer dish to your cooking basket.

9. Cook for 20 minutes.

10. Serve and enjoy!

Nutritional Contents:

- Calories: 807
- Fat: 37g
- Carbohydrates: 89g
- Protein: 13g

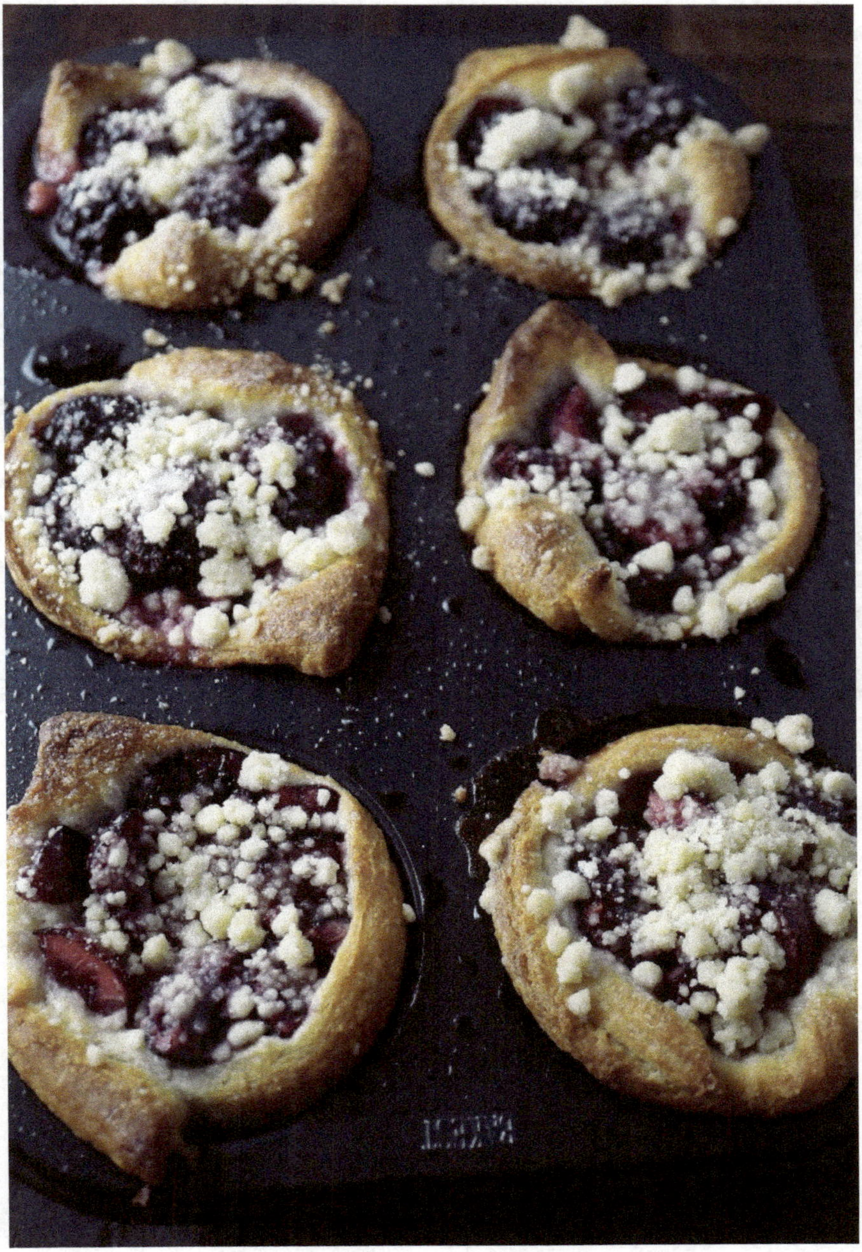

Nuts And Cocoa Bombs

Serving: 6

Prep Time: 10 minutes

Cooking Time: 8 minutes

Ingredients:

- 1 teaspoon vanilla extract
- 4 tablespoons coconut oil
- 1/3 cup swerve
- ¼ cup of cocoa powder
- 2 cups macadamia nuts

Directions:

1. Take a bowl and mix all the ingredients and whisk well.
2. Shape medium balls out of this mix, place them in your air fryer, and cook at 300°F for 8 minutes. Serve cold

Nutritional Contents:

- Calories: 120
- Fat: 12g
- Carbohydrates: 2g
- Protein: 1g

Creamy Coconut Chips

Serving: 4

Prep Time: 10 minutes

Cooking Time: 10 minutes

Ingredients:

- 3 whole eggs
- 8 ounces cream cheese, soft
- 4 tablespoons swerve
- 3 tablespoons coconut, shredded and unsweetened
- 2 tablespoons butter, melted

Directions:

1. Take a bowl and mix all the ingredients and whisk well.
2. Divide into small ramekins, put them in the fryer, and cook at 320 degrees F and bake for 10 minutes. Serve cold

Nutritional Contents:

- Calories: 614
- Fat: 4g
- Carbohydrates: 5g
- Protein: 5g

Nutritional Contents:

- Calories: 183
- Fat: 4g
- Carbohydrates: 4g
- Protein: 7g

Divine Almond Cupcakes

Serving: 4

Prep Time: 10 minutes

Cooking Time: 20 minutes

Ingredients:

- 1 teaspoon baking powder
- ½ teaspoon baking powder
- ½ teaspoon baking soda
- 1 teaspoon vanilla extract
- 4 tablespoons coconut oil, melted
- 3 tablespoons stevia
- ½ cup of cocoa powder
- ¼ cup almond milk
- 4 eggs, whisked
- ¼ cup coconut flour

Directions:

1. Take a bowl and mix all the ingredients except the cooking spray and whisk well.
2. Grease a cupcake tin that fits the air fryer with the cooking spray pour the cupcake mix put the pan in your

Air Fryer cook at 350°F for 25 minutes, cool down and serve

Nutritional Contents:

- Calories: 103
- Fat: 4g
- Carbohydrates: 6g
- Protein: 3g

Terrific Baked Plum

Serving: 4

Prep Time: 10 minutes

Cooking Time: 20 minutes

Ingredients:

- ½ teaspoon cinnamon powder
- 1 teaspoon ginger, ground
- 2 tablespoons water
- 1 lemon, zest grated
- 10 drops stevia
- 6 plums, cut into wedges

Directions:

1. In a pan that fits the Air Fryer, combine the plums with the rest of the ingredients, toss gently.
2. Put the pan in the air fryer and cook at 360°F for 20 minutes. Serve cold

Nutritional Contents:

- Calories: 170
- Fat: 5g
- Carbohydrates: 3g
- Protein: 5g

Hearty Currant Pudding

Serving: 4

Prep Time: 10 minutes

Cooking Time: 20 minutes

Ingredients:

- 1 cup red currants, blended
- 1 cup black currants, blended
- 3 tablespoons stevia
- 1 cup coconut cream

Directions:

1. In a bowl, combine all the ingredients and stir well.
2. Divide into ramekins, put them in the fryer, and cook at 340°F for 20 minutes. Serve the pudding cold.

Nutritional Contents:

- Calories: 200
- Fat: 4g
- Carbohydrates: 4g
- Protein: 6g

Spicy Avocado Pudding

Serving: 4

Prep Time: 10 minutes

Cooking Time: 25 minutes

Ingredients:

- ½ teaspoon ginger powder
- 1 teaspoon cinnamon powder
- 1 cup of coconut milk
- ¾ cup swerve
- 2 eggs, whisked
- 4 small avocados, peeled and pitted, mashed

Directions:

1. Take a bowl and mix all the ingredients and whisk well.
2. Pour into a pudding mold, put it in the air fryer, and cook at 350 degrees F for 25 minutes. Serve warm

Nutritional Contents:

- Calories: 192
- Fat: 8g
- Carbohydrates: 5g
- Protein: 4g

Authentic Chocolate Mug Cake

Serving: 4

Prep Time: 10 minutes

Cooking Time: 20 minutes

Ingredients:

- 3 tablespoons coconut oil
- 5 tablespoons caster sugar
- 3 tablespoons whole milk
- 1 tablespoon cocoa powder
- ¼ cup self-rising flour

Directions:

1. Preheat your Air fryer to 390 o F and grease a large mug lightly.
2. Mix all the ingredients in a shallow mug until well combined.
3. Arrange the mug into the Air fryer basket and cook for about 13 minutes.
4. Serve and enjoy!

Nutritional Contents:

- Calories: 729
- Fat: 40g
- Carbohydrates: 88g
- Protein: 6g

Cinnamon And Cheese Pancake

Serving: 4

Prep Time: 7 minutes

Cooking Time: 20 minutes

Ingredients:

- ½ cup brown sugar
- ½ teaspoon cinnamon
- 2 cups low fat cream cheese
- 2 whole eggs

Directions:

1. Preheat your Air Fryer to a temperature of 330 degrees F
2. Take a blender and add sugar, cheese, eggs, and cinnamon
3. Pour about ¼ of the mixture into the Air Fryer cooking basket, cook for 2 minutes per side
4. Repeat with the remaining batter
5. Serve and enjoy!

Nutritional Contents:

- Calories: 140
- Fat: 10g
- Carbohydrates: 5g
- Protein: 22g

Scallops And Dill

Serving: 4

Prep Time: 5 minutes

Cooking Time: 10 minutes

Ingredients:

- 1-pound sea scallops
- 1 tablespoon lemon juice
- 1 teaspoon dill
- 2 teaspoons olive oil
- Black pepper as needed
- Salt as needed

Directions:

1. Preheat your Air Fryer to 360 degrees F
2. Take a bowl and add oil, dill, pepper, lemon juice and stir
3. Transfer prepared scallops to Air Fryer and cook for 5 minutes
4. Divide the scallops with the dill sauce on top
5. Enjoy!

Nutritional Contents:

- Calories: 451
- Fat: 39g
- Carbohydrates: 3g
- Protein: 19g

Cheesy Bread Cups

Number of Servings: 2

Prep Time: 10 minutes

Cooking Time: 15 minutes

Ingredients:

- 2 whole eggs
- 2 tablespoons cheddar cheese, grated
- Salt and pepper to taste
- 1 ham, cut into 2 slices
- 4 bread slices, flattened with a rolling pin

Directions:

1. Preheat your Air Fryer to 300 degrees F
2. Take two ramekins and spray both with cooking spray
3. Place two slices of bread into each ramekin
4. Add ham slice pieces into each ramekin
5. Crack an egg into each ramekin, sprinkle cheese
6. Season with salt and pepper
7. Transfer to your Air Fryer cooking basket, cook for 15 minutes
8. Serve and enjoy!

Nutritional Contents:

- Calories: 162
- Fat: 8g
- Carbohydrates: 10g
- Protein: 11g

Peanut Butter And Banana Sandwich

Number of Servings: 1

Prep Time: 5 minutes

Cooking Time: 6 minutes

Ingredients:

- 2 slices whole what bread
- 1 teaspoon maple syrup
- 1 banana, sliced
- 2 tablespoons peanut butter

Directions:

1. Preheat your Air Fryer to 330 degrees F
2. Coat one side of your sliced bread with peanut butter
3. Add sliced banana to the buttered side and drizzle maple syrup
4. Transfer to Air Fryer and cook for 6 minutes
5. Serve and enjoy!

Nutritional Contents:

- Calories: 211
- Fat: 9g
- Carbohydrates: 7g
- Protein: 11g

Mini Cheeseburger Sliders

Number of Servings: 6

Prep Time: 5 minutes

Cooking Time: 10 minutes

Ingredients:

- 1-pound beef, ground
- 6 cheddar cheese slices
- 6 dinner rolls
- 6 tablespoons mayonnaise/ketchup
- Salt and pepper to taste

Directions:

1. Preheat your Air Fryer to 390 degrees F

2. Form 6 beef patties (each patty using 2.5 ounces meat) and season them with salt and pepper

3. Add burger patties to the Air Fryer cooking basket

4. Cook for 10 minutes, remove them from the Fryer

5. Top the patties with cheese slice and return to the Air Fryer, cook for 1 minute until the cheese melts

6. Slather tomato ketchup/mayonnaise generously over the top and bottom part of the dinner rolls

7. Transfer to the dinner roll, serve warm and enjoy!

Nutritional Contents:

- Calories: 262
- Fat: 10g
- Carbohydrates: 9g
- Protein: 16g

Chicken Cheese Fillet

Serving: 4

Prep Time: 5 minutes

Cooking Time: 15 minutes

Ingredients:

- 2 chicken fillets
- 4 Gouda cheese slices
- 4 ham slices
- Salt and pepper to taste
- 1 tablespoon chives, chopped

Directions:

1. Preheat your Air Fryer to 356 degrees F
2. Cut the chicken fillets into four fillets, make a horizontal slit to the edge
3. Open the fillet and season generously with salt and pepper
4. Cover each piece with chives and cheese slice
5. Close fillet, wrap them with ham slices
6. Transfer prepared fillets to Air Fryer cooking basket
7. Cook for 15 minutes
8. Serve and enjoy!

Nutritional Contents:

- Calories: 386
- Fat: 21g
- Carbohydrates: 14g
- Protein: 30g

Pineapple Pizza

Serving: 4

Prep Time: 5 minutes

Cooking Time: 10 minutes

Ingredients:

- 1 whole wheat tortilla
- ¼ cup tomato pizza sauce
- ¼ cup pineapple tidbits
- ¼ cup mozzarella cheese, grated
- ¼ cup ham slices

Directions:

1. Preheat your Air Fryer to 300 degrees F
2. Transfer tortilla on a baking sheet spread pizza sauce over tortilla
3. Arrange ham slices, cheese, pineapple over tortilla
4. Transfer the prepared pizza to Air Fryer cooking basket
5. Cook for 10 minutes
6. Serve and enjoy!

Nutritional Contents:

- Calories: 80
- Fat: 2g
- Carbohydrates: 12g
- Protein: 4g

Lovely Plum Cream

Serving: 4

Prep Time: 5 minutes

Cooking Time: 10 minutes

Ingredients:

- 1 lb. Plums pitted and chopped.
- 1 ½ cups heavy cream
- ¼ cup swerve
- 1 tbsp. lemon juice

Directions:

1. Take a bowl and mix all the ingredients and whisk well.
2. Divide this into 4 ramekins, put them in the air fryer, and cook at 340°F for 20 minutes. Serve cold

Nutritional Contents:

- Calories: 171
- Fat: 4g
- Carbohydrates: 4g
- Protein: 4g

Air Fried Spinach Fish

Serving: 4

Prep Time: 20 minutes

Cooking Time: 6 minutes

Ingredients:

- 1 cup spinach leaves, witted
- 2 tablespoons olive oil
- 1 large egg
- 4 filets perch
- 2 cups flour
- 1 teaspoon salt
- ½ teaspoon black pepper, ground
- 1 tablespoon lemon juice

Directions:

1. Preheat your Air Fryer to 370 degrees F
2. Add flour, salt, pepper, spinach, and egg in a bowl
3. Make a mixture
4. Dip each filet in the batter
5. Place them on the Air Fryer tray
6. Drizzle with olive oil
7. Cook for 12 minutes
8. Sprinkle with lemon juice
9. Serve and enjoy!

Nutritional Contents:

- Calories: 227.8
- Fat: 5.5g
- Carbohydrates: 14.7g
- Protein: 1.8g

Tandori Fish

Serving: 4

Prep Time: 25 minutes

Cooking Time: 20 minutes

Ingredients:

- 1 whole fish, such as trout
- 3 tablespoons olive oil
- ½ teaspoon turmeric, grounded
- 1 cup papaya, mashed
- 1 tablespoon garam masala seasoning
- ½ teaspoon cumin, grounded
- 1 tablespoon chili powder
- 1 teaspoon salt
- ½ teaspoon black pepper, ground
- 8 cloves garlic, minced

Directions:

1. Preheat your Air Fryer to 340 degrees F
2. Slash slits into the sides of the fish
3. Add all the remaining ingredients to make a mixture
4. Coat all sides of the fish by using the mixture
5. Place coated fish into the Air Fryer basket

6. Cook for 20 minutes

7. Serve and enjoy!

Nutritional Contents:

- Calories: 294.2
- Fat: 11g
- Carbohydrates: 21g
- Protein: 43g

Cod And Fennel Meal

Serving: 4

Prep Time: 5 minutes

Cook Time: 10 minutes

Ingredients:

- 2 cod fillets
- Salt and pepper to taste
- 1 cup grapes, halved
- ½ cup pecans
- 1 small fennel, sliced
- 3 cups kale, shredded
- 2 teaspoons balsamic vinegar
- 2 tablespoons extra virgin olive oil

Directions:

1. Pre-heat your Air Fryer to 400 degrees Fahrenheit and season your fillets with pepper and salt
2. Drizzle olive oil on top
3. Transfer the fillets to your cooking basket making sure that the skin side is facing down
4. Fry for 10 minutes and remove them once done
5. Make an aluminum tent and allow them to cool

6. Take a bowl and add grapes, pecans, fennels
7. Drizzle olive oil and season with salt and pepper
8. Add the mix to your cooking basket and cook for 5 minutes
9. Dress them with balsamic vinegar and add olive oil
10. Season with some additional pepper and salt it you need, enjoy!

Nutrition Values (Per Serving)

- Calories: 269
- Carbohydrate: 5g
- Protein: 32g
- Fat: 1g

Prawn Curry

Serving: 4

Prep Time: 15 minutes

Cooking Time: 20 minutes

Ingredients:

- 6 king prawn
- ½ teaspoon black pepper, ground
- 1 and a ½ cup of chicken broth
- 1 medium onion, finely chopped
- 2 tablespoons curry powder
- 1 teaspoon salt
- 1 tablespoon olive oil
- 1 tablespoon tomato paste
- ½ teaspoon coriander

Directions:

1. Preheat your Air Fryer to 370 degrees F
2. Season the prawns with salt and pepper
3. Cook for 7 minutes
4. Heat the olive oil in a large skillet
5. When it becomes hot, add the onion
6. Cook until soft

7. Sit in the curry, coriander and tomato paste
8. Cook then stirring for 1 minute
9. Add the chicken broth and stir
10. Serve with sauce and enjoy!

Nutritional Contents:

- Calories: 294.2
- Fat: 11g
- Carbohydrates: 21g
- Protein: 18g

Crusted Halibut

Serving: 4

Prep Time: 30 minutes

Cooking Time: 25 minutes

Ingredients:

- 4 halibut fillets
- 1 tablespoon olive oil
- 2 teaspoons lemon zest
- ¾ cup panko bread crumbs
- ¼ cup fresh dill, chopped
- ½ cup fresh parsley, chopped
- ½ teaspoon black pepper, ground
- 1 teaspoon salt

Directions:

1. Preheat your Air Fryer to 390 degrees F
2. Add all the ingredients except halibut and olive oil in your food processor
3. Pulse until you get a smooth mixture
4. Coat the halibut in the mixture
5. Then place inside the Air Fryer basket
6. Drizzle with olive oil
7. Cook for 25 minutes
8. Serve and enjoy!

Nutritional Contents:

- Calories: 454
- Fat: 15g
- Carbohydrates: 38g
- Protein: 4g

Spiced Up Air Fried Buffalo Wings

Serving: 4

Prep Time: 10 minutes

Cooking Time: 30 minutes

Ingredients:

- 4 pounds of chicken wings
- ½ cup cayenne pepper sauce
- ½ cup of coconut oil
- 1 tablespoon Worcestershire sauce
- 1 teaspoon salt

Directions:

1. Take a mixing cup and add cayenne pepper sauce, coconut oil, Worcestershire sauce, and salt
2. Mix well and keep it on the side
3. Pat the chicken dry and transfer to your Air Fryer
4. Cook for 25 minutes at 380 degrees F, making sure to shake the basket once
5. Increase the temperature to 400 degrees F and cook for 5 minutes more
6. Remove them and dump into a large-sized mixing bowl
7. Add the prepared sauce and toss well
8. Serve with celery sticks and enjoy!

Nutritional Contents:

- Calories: 244
- Fat: 20g
- Carbohydrates: 6g
- Protein: 8g

Caprese Chicken With Balsamic Sauce

Serving: 6

Prep Time: 5 minutes

Cook Time: 25 minutes

Ingredients:

- 6 chicken breasts
- 6 basil leaves
- ¼ cup balsamic vinegar
- 6 slices tomato
- 1 tablespoon butter
- 6 slices mozzarella cheese

Directions:

1. Pre-heat your Fryer to 400 degrees F.
2. Take frying and place it over medium heat, add butter and balsamic vinegar and let it melt.
3. Cover the chicken meat with the marinade.
4. Transfer chicken to your Air Fryer cooking basket and cook for 20 minutes.

5. Cover cooked chicken with basil, tomato slices, and cheese.

6. Serve and enjoy!

Nutritional Contents:

- Calories: 740
- Fat: 54g
- Carbohydrates: 4g
- Protein: 30g

Rice Flour Crusted Tofu

Serving: 4

Prep Time: 10 minutes

Cook Time: 14-20 minutes

Ingredients:

- 1: 14-oz block firm tofu, pressed and cubed into ½-inch size
- 1/4 cup rice flour
- 2 tbsp. olive oil
- 2 tbsp. cornstarch
- Salt and ground black pepper; as your liking

Directions:

1. In a bowl, mix cornstarch, rice flour, salt, and black pepper.
2. Coat the tofu evenly with flour mixture. Drizzle the tofu with oil.

3. Set the temperature of the air fryer to 360°F. Grease an air fryer basket.
4. Arrange tofu cubes into the prepared air fryer basket in a single layer.
5. Air fry for about 14 minutes per side. Remove from the air fryer and transfer the tofu onto serving plates. Serve warm.

Nutrition Contents:

- Calories: 660
- Fat: 30g
- Carbohydrates: 83g
- Protein: 19g

Healthy Croissant Rolls

Serving: 8

Prep Time: 10 minutes

Cook Time: 2-5 minutes

Ingredients:

- 1 (8 ounces can) croissant rolls
- 4 tablespoons butter, melted

Directions:

1. Set the temperature of air fryer to 320 degrees F. Grease an air fryer basket.
2. Arrange croissant rolls into the prepared air fryer basket.
3. Air fry for about 4 minutes.
4. Flip the side and air fry for 1-2 more minutes.
5. Remove from the air fryer and transfer onto a platter.
6. Drizzle with the melted butter and serve hot.

Nutrition Contents:

- Calories: 152
- Fat: 10g
- Carbohydrates: 11g
- Protein: 2g

Cheesy Mushroom Pizza

Serving: 4

Prep Time: 15 minutes

Cook Time: 5 minutes

Ingredients:

- 2 Portobello mushroom caps stemmed
- 2 tablespoons olive oil
- 1/8 teaspoon dried Italian seasonings
- Salt, to taste
- 2 tablespoons canned tomatoes, chopped
- 2 tablespoons mozzarella cheese, shredded
- 2 Kalamata olives, pitted and sliced
- 2 tablespoons Parmesan cheese, grated freshly
- 1 teaspoon red pepper flakes, crushed

Directions:

1. Set the temperature of air fryer to 320 degrees F. Grease an air fryer basket.

2. With a spoon, scoop out the center of each mushroom cap.
3. Coat each mushroom cap with oil from both sides.
4. Sprinkle the inside of caps with Italian seasoning and salt.
5. Place the canned tomato evenly over both caps, followed by the olives and mozzarella cheese.
6. Arrange mushroom caps into the prepared air fryer basket.
7. Air fry for about 5-6 minutes.
8. Remove from the air fryer and immediately sprinkle with the Parmesan cheese and red pepper flakes.
9. Serve.

Nutrition Contents:

- Calories: 251
- Fat: 21g
- Carbohydrates: 5g
- Protein: 13g

Chinese Mushroom Tilapia

Serving: 4

Prep Time: 20 minutes

Cooking Time: 16 minutes

Ingredients:

- ½ cup yellow onion, sliced thin
- 4 ounces filets tilapia
- 2 tablespoons olive oil
- 2 cups mushroom, sliced
- 4 tablespoons soy sauce
- 2 cloves garlic, minced
- 1 tablespoon honey
- 2 tablespoons rice vinegar
- 2 and ½ teaspoon salt
- 1 tablespoon red chili flakes

Directions:

1. Preheat your Air Fryer to 350 degrees F
2. Season the fish with half the salt
3. Drizzle with half the oil
4. Cook for 15 minutes
5. Take a large skillet and add remaining oil and heat it

6. Add the onion, garlic, and mushroom when it is hot

7. Cook until onions are soft

8. Stir in the soy sauce, honey, vinegar, and chili flakes

9. Simmer for 1 minute

10. Serve with mushroom sauce and enjoy!

Nutritional Contents:

- Calories: 57
- Fat: 3.5g
- Carbohydrates: 1.7g
- Protein: 1.8g

Air Fried Dragon Shrimp

Serving: 4

Prep Time: 15 minutes

Cooking Time: 10 minutes

Ingredients:

- 1 pound raw shrimp, peeled and deveined
- A ½ cup of soy sauce
- 2 eggs
- 2 tablespoons olive oil
- 1 cup yellow onion, diced
- ¼ cup flour
- ½ teaspoon red pepper, ground
- ½ teaspoon ginger, grounded

Directions:

1. Preheat your Air Fryer to 350 degrees F
2. Add all the ingredients except for the shrimp to make the batter
3. Set it aside for 10 minutes
4. Dip each shrimp into the batter to coat all sides
5. Place them on the Air Fryer basket
6. Cook for 10 minutes
7. Serve and enjoy!

Nutritional Contents:

- Calories: 221
- Fat: 13g
- Carbohydrates: 1g
- Protein: 23g

Stuffed Breadcrumbs Mushrooms

Serving: 4

Prep Time: 10 minutes

Cook Time: 25 minutes

Ingredients:

- 16 small button mushrooms, stemmed and gills removed
- 1 garlic clove; crushed
- 1 ½ spelt bread slices
- 1 tbsp. flat-leaf parsley, finely chopped
- 1 ½ tbsp. olive oil
- Salt and ground black pepper; as your liking

Directions:

1. In a food processor, add the bread slices and pulse until fine crumbs form. Transfer the crumbs into a bowl. Add the garlic, parsley, salt, and black pepper and stir to combine.
2. Stir in the olive oil. Set the temperature of the air fryer to 390°F. Grease an air fryer basket.
3. Stuff each mushroom cap with the breadcrumbs mixture .
4. Arrange mushroom caps into the prepared air fryer basket. Air fry for about 9 to 10 minutes.
5. Remove from the air fryer and transfer the mushrooms onto a serving platter.
6. Set aside to cool slightly. Serve warm.

Nutrition Contents:

- Calories: 751
- Fat: 31g
- Carbohydrates: 97g
- Protein: 15g

Basil Dip And Assorted Roast Vegetable

Serving: 2

Prep Time: 10 minutes

Cook Time: 10-15 minutes

Ingredients:

- 12 cherry tomatoes
- 3 slender zucchini, sliced into ½ inch thick rounds, cut into 24 pieces
- Salt as needed
- ¼ cup olive oil
- 1 onion, quartered and cut into 24 pieces
- 2 red bell pepper, cut into 1-inch pieces, 12 pieces total

Basil dip

- ½ teaspoon salt
- ½ cup basil
- ½ cup extra virgin olive oil
- 1 cup zucchini, diced
- ½ cup raw walnuts

Directions:

1. Preheat your Toaster Oven to 380 degrees F in Air Fry mode
2. Thread veggies into small skewers (small enough to fit in cooking basket)in a uniform pattern, place them on parchment pattern
3. The pattern should be tomatoes between 2 veggies
4. Apply oil all over and season well
5. Roast for 10-15 minutes
6. Once done, add dip ingredients to a food processor and process well
7. Add more olive oil if needed
8. Serve veggies with dip
9. Enjoy!

Nutritional Contents:

- Calories: 112
- Fat: 10g
- Carbohydrates: 4g
- Protein: 1g

Warm Chickpea Burger

Serving: 4

Prep Time: 10 minutes

Cook Time: 10-15 minutes

Ingredients:

- 3 cups cooked chickpeas
- 1 cup kale, chopped
- 1 teaspoon cayenne
- 2 onions, chopped
- Salt as needed
- 1/3 cup dry quinoa
- ¼ cup chickpea flour
- 2 teaspoons oregano, dill and basil
- Springwater as needed

Directions:

1. Take a hot pan and toast in the hot pan, cook well
2. Once quinoa has separated, add 2/3 of 1 cup water to the pan and bring to boil
3. Cover tight with lid and give quinoa fifteen minutes to cook over low heat
4. Remove heat and let it sit for 10 minutes
5. Mash chickpeas in a large bowl
6. Add cooked quinoa, chopped kale, chickpea flour, seasoning, cayenne, and salt
7. Add water if needed
8. Preheat your Toaster Oven to 350 degrees F in Air Fry mode
9. Make patties and transfer them to Toaster Oven cooking basket
10. Brush with a thin layer of oil, bake for 10-15 minutes until done
11. Serve and enjoy!

Nutritional Contents:

- Calories: 145
- Fat: 2g
- Carbohydrates: 24g
- Protein: 8g

Exceptional Spaghetti Squash Roast

Serving: 4

Prep Time: 10 minutes

Cook Time: 20-25 minutes

Ingredients:

- 1 spaghetti squash, cut half, lengthwise
- 1 and ½ tablespoons olive oil
- 1 garlic clove, minced
- 1 small zucchini, chopped
- 6 tomatoes, diced
- 1 cup chickpeas, cooked
- ½ teaspoon oregano
- ½ teaspoon salt
- 1 cup basil, torn
- ½ teaspoon zest, lemon

Directions:

1. Preheat your Toaster Oven to 350 degrees F in Air Fry mode
2. Rub 1 tablespoon olive oil on each end of spaghetti squash halves, press them down on the cooking basket
3. Cook for 20-30 minutes
4. Take a skillet and add remaining ½ tablespoon olive oil, add garlic, tomato, zucchini
5. Cook for 8 minutes
6. Add chickpeas, oregano, cook for 3-4 minutes and season
7. Remove squash from fryer and use a fork to stroke lengthwise and separate the flesh
8. Add veggies, chickpea mix, and stir
9. Top with basil, drizzle olive oil and zest
10. Enjoy!

Nutritional Contents:

- Calories: 253
- Fat: 20 g
- Carbohydrates: 12 g
- Protein: 8g

Spiced Up Orange Bowl

Serving: 2

Prep Time: 10 minutes

Cook Time: 20-25 minutes

Ingredients:

- 2 teaspoons sesame seed oil
- 1 date, pitted and soaked
- 3 tablespoons orange juice
- 1 tablespoon tamari
- 1 garlic clove, grated
- ½ teaspoon red chili flakes
- ½ teaspoon ginger, grated
- ½ teaspoon ginger, grated
- 1 tablespoon sesame seeds
- 2 cups zucchini, cubed

Directions:

1. Preheat your Toaster Oven to 380 degrees F
2. Add zucchini in cooking basket and drizzle oil on top
3. Roast for 10-20 minutes
4. Take your blender and add date, juice, tamari, garlic, flakes, ginger and pulse well
5. Put cooked zucchini to a skillet and add orange juice mixture to the pan, cook on a low simmer for 2-3 minutes until reduced
6. Serve and enjoy with a garnish of sesame seeds
7. Enjoy!

Nutritional Contents:

- Calories: 165
- Fat: 13g
- Carbohydrates: 10g
- Protein: 6g

Exquisite Squash Salad

Serving: 3

Prep Time: 10 minutes

Cook Time: 30-40 minutes

Ingredients:

- 1 small butternut squash, cubed
- 2 small apples, cored and chopped
- 2 tablespoons avocado oil
- ¼ teaspoon cinnamon
- 1/8 teaspoon oregano
- 1 teaspoon salt
- 1 teaspoon pepper
- 1 tablespoon walnuts, toasted and chopped
- 1 tablespoon parsley

Directions:

1. Preheat your Toaster Oven to 380 degrees F in Air Fry mode
2. Line a baking tray with parchment paper
3. Take a large bowl and add all ingredients except parsley and nuts
4. Spread on the tray
5. Transfer to Toaster Oven cooking basket, roast for 30-40 minutes
6. Serve and enjoy with a sprinkle of walnuts and parsley
7. Serve and enjoy!

Nutritional Contents:

- Calories: 128
- Fat: 11g
- Carbohydrates: 6g
- Protein: 3g